HALLOWEEN CLASSICS FOR 2

ARRANGED BY KEVIN OLSON

ISBN 978-1-70516-861-5

HAL•LEONARD®

Visit Hal Leonard Online at
www.halleonard.com

World headquarters, contact:
Hal Leonard
7777 West Bluemound Road
Milwaukee, WI 53213
Email: info@halleonard.com

In Europe, contact:
Hal Leonard Europe Limited
1 Red Place
London, W1K 6PL
Email: info@halleonardeurope.com

In Australia, contact:
Hal Leonard Australia Pty. Ltd.
4 Lentara Court
Cheltenham, Victoria, 3192 Australia
Email: info@halleonard.com.au

Danse Macabre

SECONDO

Camille Saint-Saëns
1835–1921
Arranged by Kevin Olson

Quickly; in one ($\dotted{} = c.\ 60$)

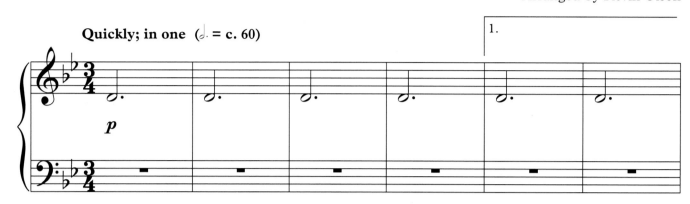

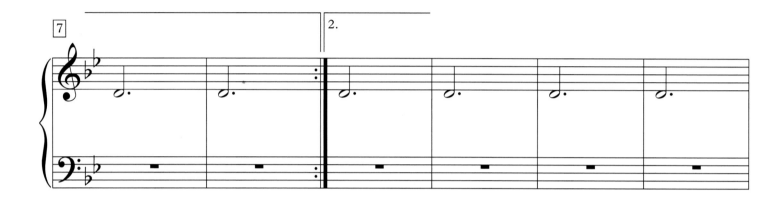

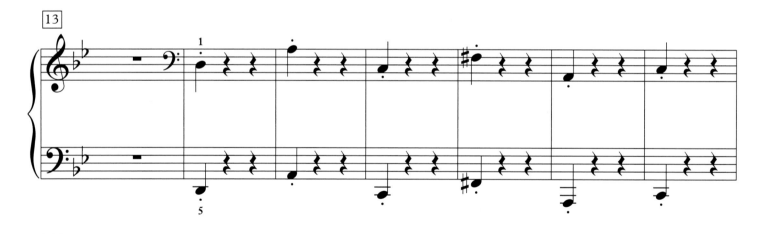

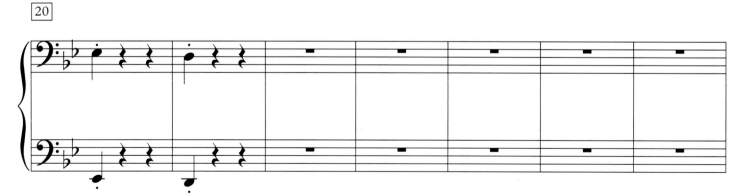

Danse Macabre

PRIMO

Camille Saint-Saëns
1835–1921
Arranged by Kevin Olson

Funeral March
from PIANO SONATA NO. 2, OP. 35

SECONDO

Frédéric Chopin
1810–1849
Arranged by Kevin Olson

Funeral March
from PIANO SONATA NO. 2, OP. 35

PRIMO

Frédéric Chopin
1810–1849
Arranged by Kevin Olson

Heavy and sustained (♩ = c. 60)

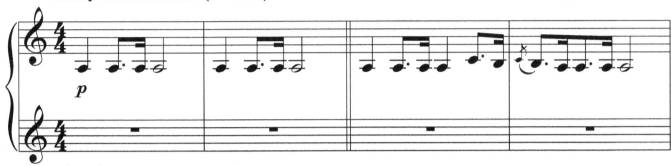

Funeral March of a Marionette

SECONDO

Charles Gounod
1818–1893
Arranged by Kevin Olson

Funeral March of a Marionette

PRIMO

Charles Gounod
1818–1893
Arranged by Kevin Olson

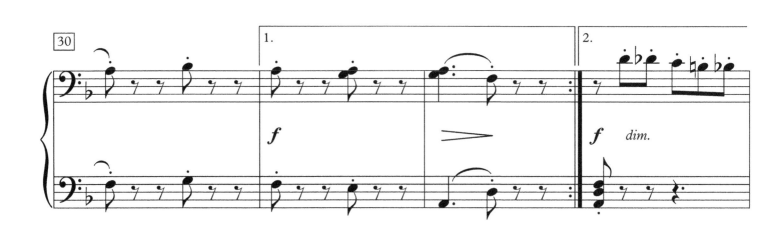

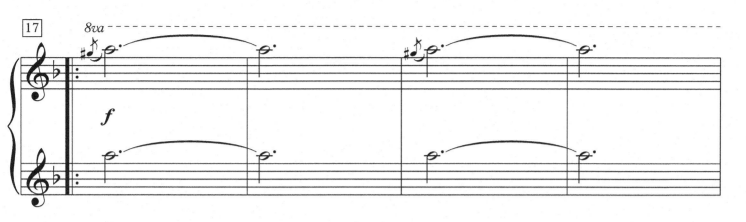

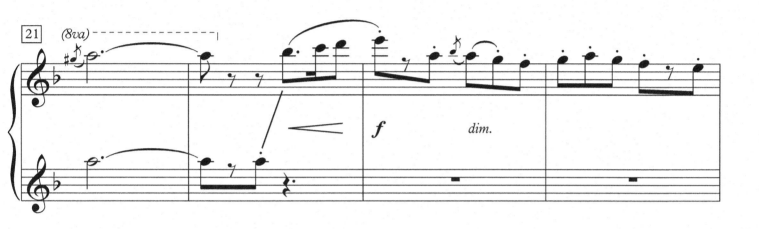

In the Hall of the Mountain King

SECONDO

Edvard Grieg
1847–1907
Arranged by Kevin Olson

Slow March; gradually getting faster

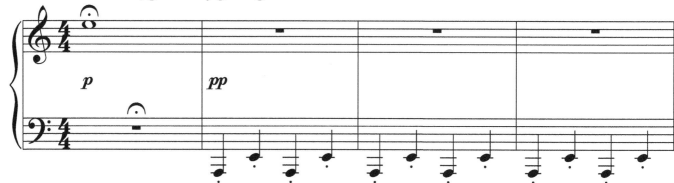

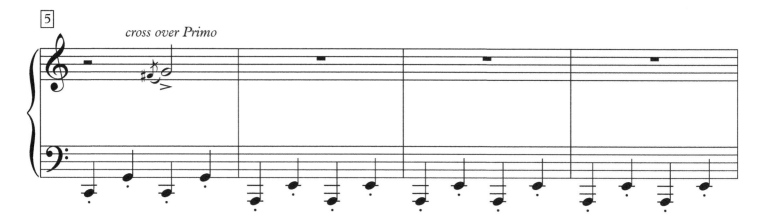

cross over Primo

cross over Primo

In the Hall of the Mountain King

PRIMO

Edvard Grieg
1847–1907
Arranged by Kevin Olson

Slow March; gradually getting faster

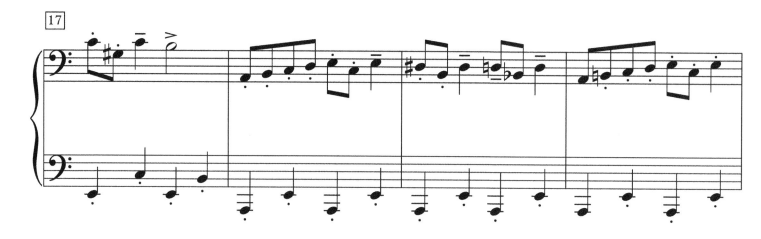

A little faster

Faster

As fast as possible

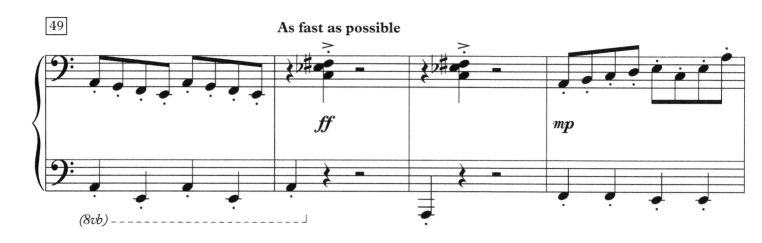

As fast as possible

Lacrymosa

from Requiem, K. 626

SECONDO

Wolfgang Amadeus Mozart
1756–1791
Arranged by Kevin Olson

Lacrymosa
from Requiem, K. 626

PRIMO

Wolfgang Amadeus Mozart
1756–1791
Arranged by Kevin Olson

Night on Bald Mountain

SECONDO

Modest Mussorgsky
1839–1881
Arranged by Kevin Olson

Night on Bald Mountain

PRIMO

Modest Mussorgsky
1839–1881
Arranged by Kevin Olson

Allegro con fuoco ($\quarternote$ = c. 144)

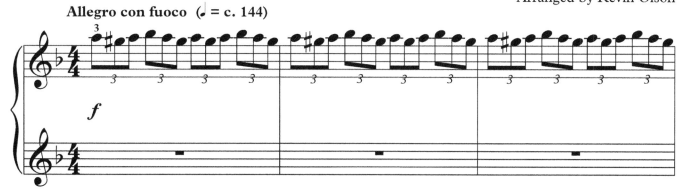

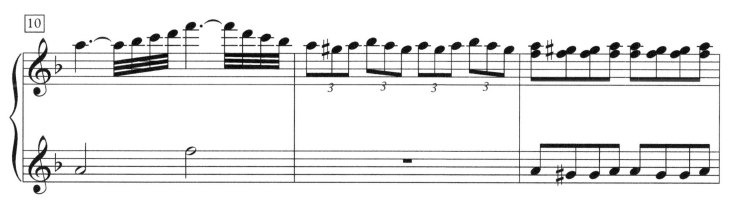

38

SECONDO

Ride of the Valkyries
from DIE WALKÜRE

SECONDO

Richard Wagner
1813–1883
Arranged by Kevin Olson

Ride of the Valkyries
from DIE WALKÜRE

PRIMO

Richard Wagner
1813–1883
Arranged by Kevin Olson

SECONDO

The Sorcerer's Apprentice

SECONDO

Paul Dukas
1865–1935
Arranged by Kevin Olson

The Sorcerer's Apprentice

PRIMO

Paul Dukas
1865–1935
Arranged by Kevin Olson

Toccata in D Minor
BWV 565

SECONDO

Johann Sebastian Bach
1685–1750
Arranged by Kevin Olson

Toccata in D Minor

BWV 565

PRIMO

Johann Sebastian Bach
1685–1750
Arranged by Kevin Olson

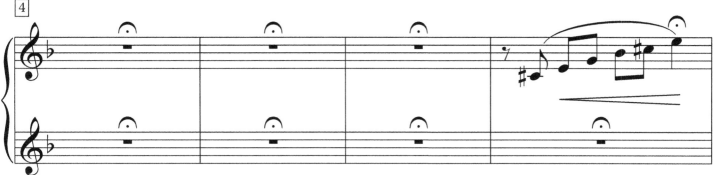

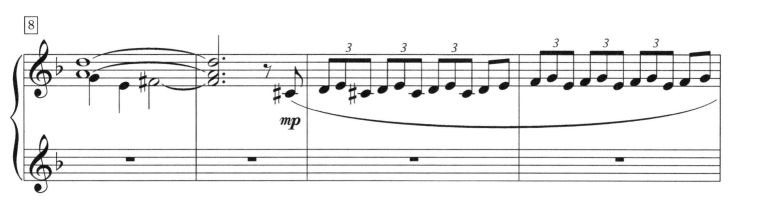

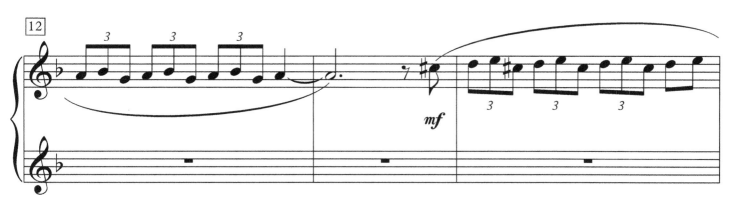

ALSO BY KEVIN OLSON

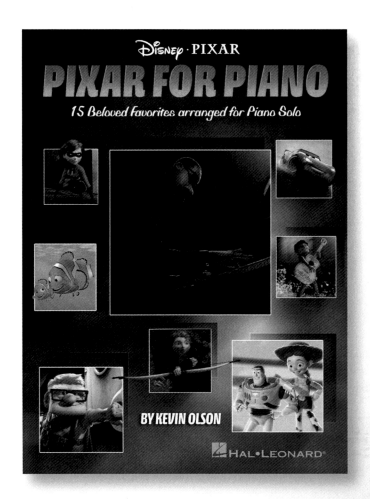

Kevin Olson is a pianist, composer, and member of the piano faculty at Utah State University, where he teaches piano literature, pedagogy, accompanying, music theory, commercial composition, and rock & roll history. Dr. Olson coordinates the piano program at Utah State and oversees the Utah State University Youth Conservatory, which provides piano instruction to over 150 pre-college community students.

A native of Utah, he began composing at age five. He has written music commissioned and performed by groups such as the Five Browns, American Piano Quartet, Chicago a cappella, and the Rich Matteson Jazz Festival. In addition to maintaining a large studio of students with varying ages and abilities, he has also presented workshops and performed in India, China, Canada, and the United Kingdom.

For more information, visit www.kevinolson.com.